Memory Lane
Tyneside

Memory Lane Tyneside

Photographs from the archives of the Evening Chronicle

Evening **Chronicle**

The Breedon Books
Publishing Company
Derby

First published in Great Britain by

The Breedon Books Publishing Company Limited

Breedon House, 44 Friar Gate, Derby, DE1 1DA.

2000

To purchase copies of photographs in this book, please telephone the Newcastle Chronicle and Journal Photo Sales Department on 0191 201 6001 for an order form.

ISBN 1 85983 201 6

Printed and bound by Butler & Tanner Ltd., Selwood Printing Works, Caxton Road, Frome, Somerset.

Colour separations and jacket printing by GreenShires Group Ltd, Leicester.

Contents

Introduction

NEWCASTLE is far more than just that distinctive bridge across one of Britain's mightiest rivers – or merely another northern city whose growth came about with the reign of King Coal and the birth of the Victorian steam-powered age of the Industrial Revolution.

So *Evening Chronicle* journalist Peter Fairley wrote in 1995 when introducing *Images of Tyneside*, the best-selling local book which comprised some of the best photographic images from the *Chronicle's* archives.

Now, at the start of another century, another millennium, we have again dipped into the newspaper's unique library of life on Tyneside through the last 100 years. As the new era gets under way it somehow seems appropriate to look back, perhaps just a little misty-eyed, at how things were on Tyneside, both long ago and with memories from such not-so-distant times.

One would have thought that the original book would have appealed almost entirely to older readers, but it was pored over avidly by a much wider age group. While evoking memories for the people who remember Tyneside as it was 30, 40, 50,

60 and more years ago, it also proved of great interest to younger people who wanted to know how their city and region looked before they were born.

This second selection of photographs, which forms *Memory Lane Tyneside*, is equally as fascinating as the first. Places and faces from a bygone age leap out to both inform and entertain and, as much as anything, underline the huge importance of a newspaper to its community, recording everyday life for the enjoyment and education of future generations.

While every care has been taken to ensure that captions are entirely accurate, one has to acknowledge that with the passage of time details have sometimes been lost. Of course, every photograph tells its own story and offers a fascinating glimpse of how life, fashions, transport and the very streets were at the time when the photographers captured them for ever on film.

This book was never intended to be a history of Tyneside – it would take several volumes to accomplish that – rather that it is an historical entertainment that we hope you will enjoy.

City Scenes

Newcastle Quay in 1928 with the newly-opened Tyne Bridge proudly spanning the river.

Newcastle Quayside at the end of the 19th century when sailing ships still lined the quay.

Grey's Monument decorated for the visit of King Edward VII to Newcastle in 1906. Almost every citizen seems to be in their Sunday best.

More loyal greetings. This time Northumberland Street is decked out for King George V's silver jubilee in 1935.

People could take their time when crossing the top of Northumberland Street before World War One. Apart from a couple of carriages there are no vehicles in sight.

Newcastle Central Railway Station and the grandeur of Neville Street in the days before World War One.

Three Newcastle men pause to look at the camera in Grainger Street around 1910 as electric trams rattle by.

Another view up Grainger Street *c*.1910. Once again trams are the main traffic.

In 1900, though, the horse was still king of the road and the two in the foreground of this photograph are pulling a tram along Grainger Street to the Central Station.

The corner of New Bridge Street and Pilgrim Street in about 1925. The corner shop is J. J. Grant, jeweller, while above are the offices of Edward Watson, estate agent.

Property at the corner of Market Street and Pilgrim Street when demolition was begun in 1929 to clear the site for the city's new police courts.

The corner of Blackett Street and Pilgrim Street in May 1935, decorated for the silver jubilee of King George V.

Silver Street, in lower Pilgrim Street, pictured just after the end of World War One. Once the haunt of coiners and thieves, within ten years it was demolished to make way for the Tyne Bridge.

Darn Crook in February 1931, with lorries transporting meat, vegetables, beer and household goods.

Barras Bridge, looking north, in November 1928. Eldon Street is on the left-hand side, in about the centre of the picture.

Barras Bridge, one of Newcastle's busiest junctions, seen here on a rainy day in November 1933.

Handyside's Buildings in Percy Street, built by William Handyside, were 25 years old when this photograph was taken in November 1928.

The Bigg Market in 1910 with shoppers thronging a traffic-free roadway.

Another view of the Bigg Market before the tram lines were laid down and before motor cars took over.

Newcastle Town Hall pictured in the 1930s. As war loomed, a suggestion was made that the tower should be pulled down to avert the danger of falling masonry during air-raids.

In July 1919, buildings in Grainger Street were adorned with flags of the nations victorious in World War One.

St Nicholas's Square with St Nicholas's Cathedral out of view on the right and Mosley Street in the background. Centre left is the memorial fountain to the temperance movement which was removed to the Bigg Market in 1902.

Christmas 1960 and workmen cover up mud with ashes at the car park on the Town Hall site near St Thomas's Church.

Heaton Road in the 1900s when two horse-drawn carts constituted a traffic jam.

The Friary, part of a warren of back streets which housed some of Newcastle's worst slums before World War One.

Flooded walkway to the outside toilets at The Willows, Red Row, in November 1955.

Newcastle prison pictured in September 1925, on the site of Carliol Square.

The people who lived here in Bermondsey Street in 1960 claimed that they endured the most primitive living conditions in Newcastle. Some of the houses were so unhygienic, they were a danger to health.

Akenside Hill in 1921. A single bed in the lodging house (in the right of this picture) cost three-halfpence a night.

Prefabs in Edward Street in April 1955.

In 1950, this prefab tenant on the Blakelaw Estate made imaginative use of a rustic fence.

Work is under way, in 1959, on twin 12-storey blocks of flats overlooking Cruddas Park on Scottswood Road. The scheme covered a site originally occupied by St Vincent's Orphanage.

Shoppers cross Blackett Street in September 1974.

In 1960, *Evening Chronicle* photographer John Nash recorded this study of an archway of the railway viaduct spanning The Side and Dean Street. St Nicholas's Cathedral stands high in the background.

Eldon Square in January 1975, overlooked by builders' scaffolding.

In 1971, young people enjoy a concert given by the musical group Bullfrog in Eldon Square.

Further back in time, in April 1953 to be exact, these mums and their children enjoyed the spring sunshine on the 'floral mile' section of the Great North Road.

Northumberland Street in June 1996. The clock and statue were restored the following year at a cost of £25,000.

Around and About

Wickham Front Street in the early 1900s, when a pony and cart was just about the only traffic the villagers ever saw.

This ramshackle collection of shops stood in Gateshead around the turn of the last century.

Coatsworth Road, Gateshead, on a summer's day around 1909.

Church Street, Gateshead, in the late 1920s, looking much the same as it had done in the years before World War One.

Pipewellgate, Gateshead, in 1927, showing the offices and works of Bretts.

The old village pump at Low Fell was still working when this photograph was taken in March 1931.

The toll house at the Gateshead end of the Redheugh Bridge in September 1934.

South Shields Market Place in 1900 with market stalls in the foreground and a pleasure fair behind.

This was the scene near the North Shields ferry landing in the 1920s.

North Shields Fish Quay in 1910, when there was still plenty of sail to be seen among the working vessels.

The central gateway of Clifford's Fort, North Shields. Once used by the War Office, in November 1928 it was being converted for use by the local fishing industry.

This photograph was taken in the back streets of North Shields in the late 1920s.

In November 1933 it was announced that tenants from the Clive Street area, pictured here, were to be moved into new council houses on the Ridges Farm Estate.

In February 1935 this shop in North Shields was claimed to be the smallest in England. It was owned by Mrs Sally Walker and was so small that no customer could actually get into the shop. They had to be served through the half-door.

In April 1932, Manor House, Tynemouth, a familiar landmark to residents and visitors for generations, was due to be demolished to make way for new building works.

Whitley Bay pictured in May 1956 when big changes were planned in the hope that it would one day rival Blackpool as a holiday resort. Lack of investment ruined those dreams.

This architect's model showed plans for a solarium at Whitley Bay.

Grasmere Place, Gosforth, pictured in September 1950. The attractive lay-out of the estate was applauded by many.

Crowds gather on the Market Place at Hexham in the early 1900s.

The ancient stone of St Wilfred's Gate in Morpeth forms a nice framework for the motor car and pedestrians in the early 1920s.

Bridge Street, Morpeth in the mid-1930s.

Stepping stones over the river at Morpeth in February 1938.

Walbottle Hall, near Newcastle, in May 1929 when it was the home of Sir Alfred and Lady Appleby.

Shopping Around

Bedlington Co-op in Edwardian times, when formally-dressed shop assistants served local womenfolk.

Bargain hunters queue outside Fenwick's in Brunswick Place in July 1957, waiting for the doors to open and the sale to begin.

Another long queue, this time for John Farnon's sale in July 1958. It was billed as 'The Great Farnon Sale'.

When this photograph was taken in December 1972, this fishmonger's shop in the Haymarket was the only one in Newcastle to specialise in squid, octopus, conger eel, sea bream, sea bass, turbot, gurnet and even shark. The manager pictured is Robert Wilson-Wardle.

Housewives at the Co-op in 1959. The 'divi' was 1s 4d in the £. Butter, lard and cheese were hand cut and no one seemed to mind that garden fertiliser was stored above open fresh food.

The day many people looked forward to – shoppers visit the Co-op offices for the pay-out of dividend.

Market Street in 1912. Bainbridge's, Newcastle's oldest department store opened in 1838, is seen here with gas lamps over the display windows. Bainbridge's moved to the Eldon Square shopping complex in 1976 and Binns took over the building before they closed their store there in 1995.

There was nothing like the old corner shop and in 1955 two members of the recently-arrived Smolinski family from Poland enjoyed friendly service at this Newcastle corner shop.

The MetroCentre at the dawn of the 21st century seems light years away from the corner shop which endured for the previous 100 years and more. In this picture, though, the place is unrecognisable as work gets under way on phase one.

John Hall opens the bubbly and toasts his workers during work on phase two of the MetroCentre.

World of Work

During World War One, women took on many unfamiliar jobs as men went to war. These lady window cleaners are busy in Newcastle *c.*1915.

There must have been some upset tummies in Newcastle in the years after World War One, as this convoy of lorries from the Scott and Turner depot seems to indicate. They were delivering supplies of Andrews Liver Salts.

Jennings the North-East motor traders' site at Bridge Street, Morpeth. They had already come a long way from their humble beginnings in a garden shed.

Women at Malling's Pottery, working on ware for King George V's silver jubilee in 1935.

In September 1936 these Newcastle women were producing ware for the following year's Coronation of King George VI.

Silksworth miners receive pocket money out of lodge funds to enable them to better enjoy the Miners' Gala in July 1952.

In March 1973, it was smiles all round when miners from two Durham pits – Kibblesworth and Ravensworth Ann – linked up 500ft underground. Unfortunately it meant 80 miners were made redundant when the neighbouring colliers joined forces.

Miners from the record-breaking Havannah Drift Colliery in Dinnington, Northumberland, start their shift in February 1975. The 570 men at the pit had broken a 13-year record by turning out 58.6 cwt of coal per man shift.

In November 1979, miners at Easington Colliery check in for the pithead ballot which will determine whether the NUM will back their national executive's rejection of the Coal Board's offer of a 20 per cent pay increase.

A steam engine destined for the LMS Railway is checked over at the Scotswood works of Armstrong Whitworth in September 1935.

In February 1939 these workers at Vickers Armstrong's Elswick Works were probably assembling gun turrets for battleships.

Management inspecting a vehicle at Vickers Armstrong Works in Newcastle in September 1959.

Welders at work on the base of an American dragline excavator at Widdington opencast site in January 1954.

In 1928 the new Riverside Quay at the Albert Edward Dock in North Shields was opened and featured this huge coal elevator

Work on the Tyne Bridge which is just taking shape in 1928.

Almost there! The two halves of the Tyne Bridge are moving slowly towards each other.

A dramatic sunset over one of the Tyne's shipyards in January 1948.

We've got a giant tanker at the bottom of our road! This 230,000-ton tanker the *Esso Northumbria* – then the largest ship ever built in Britain – will soon be launched by 18-year-old Princess Anne in May 1969 at Wallsend. It was built by Swan Hunter and Tyne Shipbuilders.

More tears than cheers. Workers watch as *HMS Richmond* slips into the Tyne in April 1993. It was the end of an era, the end of 2,000 years of shipbuilding on Tyneside.

Consett steelworkers march through the streets of London in July 1980, protesting at the closure the steelworks and the effect this would have on their community.

It was all in vain. The last shift leaves Consett on 12 September 1980.

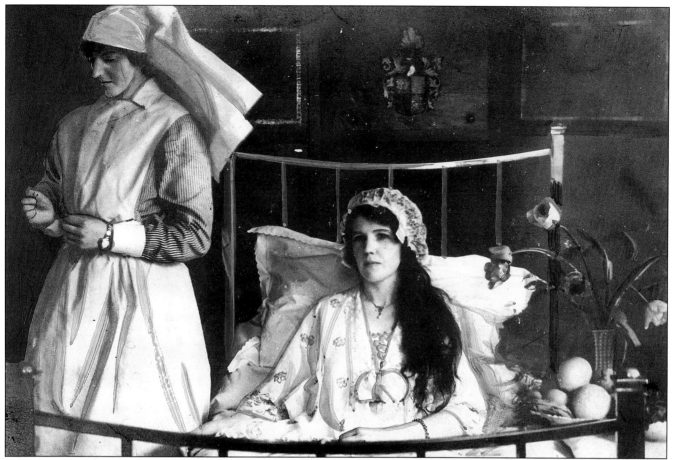

A scene in the old Maternity Hospital in New Bridge Street, in the building later occupied by the BBC.

This horse-drawn ambulance was used at Walker Gate Hospital as late as 1922.

Some of the nurses who worked at St Nicholas's Hospital in 1949.

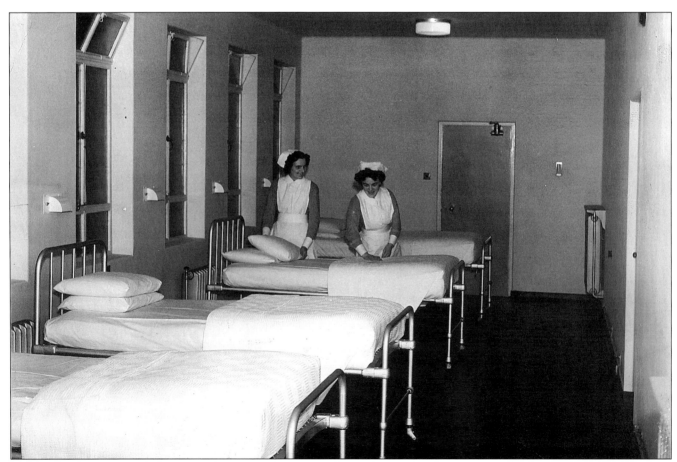

Nurses busy at St Nicholas's Hospital in December 1950. This is the insulin department of the recently-opened Interim Treatment Centre.

Health workers protesting outside the Fleming Hospital in May 1976 when it was threatened by Government cuts.

The new Freeman Road Hospital in June 1977. There had been fears that it would have to be 'mothballed' due to Government cuts.

Transports of Delight

The Armstrong Whitworth car factory on Tyneside in 1911. By the outbreak of World War One the factory was producing 16 different models for those who could afford them.

Workmen painting white lines on the road at a notorious local accident blackspot where Benfield Road and Red Hall Drive run into the Coast Road. This photograph was taken in July 1955.

In this picture taken in 1970 there is a remarkable absence of traffic in Grainger Street on a Friday afternoon.

The main portal of the Tyne Tunnel at Howden in August 1962.

Work is almost complete on the Tyne Tunnel.

Tram cars line up at Gosforth Racecourse in 1909, ready to take racegoers home at the end of the meeting.

Children's special tramcar at Saltwell Park in 1936.

Newcastle's first motor bus, seen here on the Westerhope run in 1912.

A Sentinel steam bus pictured on Tyneside just after the end of World War One.

A bus outing about 1924, near St James's Park. Note the young man with the accordion.

A Daimler bus ready for a Tyneside school run before World War Two.

This Wrekenton-bound bus is the first to cross the Tyne Bridge after the switch from trams in 1950.

In March 1964 these trolley buses were left stranded in the rain in Grainger Street after overhead power lines snapped.

After its run from Newcastle through Gosforth and Callerton this two-coach train is at Ponteland Station in the early 1900s before its engine is turned around and it makes the return journey.

These happy travellers are pictured at Newcastle Central Station in the early 1930s.

Backgrounds ancient and modern. The *Flying Scotsman* express approaches Newcastle Central Station in August 1932 on its non-stop run from Edinburgh to London. The ancient Newcastle Keep and the then new Tyne Bridge form an impressive backdrop.

A1 locomotive no. 569 is ready to head north from Newcastle Central Station in 1934.

August 1960 – flashback to the days when Consett had its own railway station.

Steam train at the diamond crossing at the east end of Newcastle Central Station, reputedly the biggest of its kind in the world. It was to be replaced by a series of points in a £31.4 million scheme.

The *Mauritania* steams out of the Tyne on her final trials in 1906. From 1909 to 1929 the vessel held the record for the fastest transatlantic crossing.

The 'Tulip Special', taking *Evening Chronicle* readers to Amsterdam in the early 1930s.

Claude Grahame-White, the pioneer airmen, in the seat of the aeroplane he brought to Gosforth Park in 1910.

In June 1955 these passengers have just disembarked from a BKS service at Newcastle Airport.

Crowds queue to inspect aircraft at the *Evening Chronicle*-sponsored open day at Newcastle Airport in July 1973.

In August 1976, hundreds of holiday-bound Geordies found themselves sweltering at Newcastle Airport after a work-to-rule meant long delays when they should have been sunning themselves in Spain.

In May 1919, Airship R-33 flew over Tynemouth Harbour. Components for the airship had been made at the Armstrong-Whitworth factory in Newcastle.

A stretch of tunnel nearing completion on the Tyne and Wear Metro Service which was officially opened by the Queen in November 1981.

Construction work in the heart of Newcastle on the Monument Station. Massive caverns were carved out from under the city to site the Metro stations as men worked day and night in a subterranean world.

In August 1980, the first Metro trains ran between Tynemouth and Haymarket. Here crowds take advantage of the rapid transport system.

Accidents do happen. The scene at Brunton Lane crossing when a Metro train crashed into a bus. Fortunately, no one was badly injured.

Tyneside at War

World War One recruiting poster to remind people that it wasn't just soldiers that were needed. Munitions factories, too, had a vital role to play.

Wreckage on Tyneside after a German air-raid in 1915. This is all that was left of the South Shields fair.

September 1939 and these young men are waiting for interviews at the Maple Street Recruiting Office.

Two men wearing gas masks have an audience during ARP exercises in the Scottswood Road area in 1939.

A crowd of excited young-sters watch the delivery of the first consignments of air-raid shelters in the Two Ball Lonnen area of Newcastle.

Residents of Links Avenue, Monkseaton, work on the first trench of the air-raid shelter which they have decided to build.

In September 1939 work was underway to protect Newcastle's public buildings with sandbags.

Workers at the Vickers-Armstrong factory at Scotswood are busy sandbagging their works.

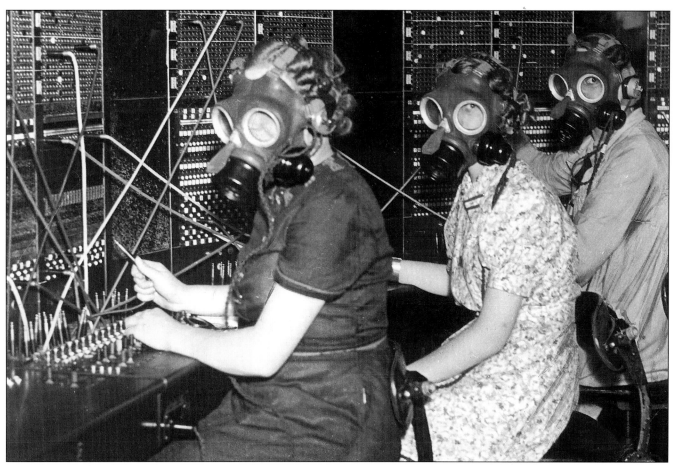

Whitley Bay telephone girls training while wearing gas masks.

Wallsend schoolchildren of Richardson Dees School setting out for Ponteland District during the evacuation of their school in September 1939.

This party of evacuees and their mums look happy enough at Percy Main as they wait for their train.

Children of All Saints' School, Gateshead, arrive at Gateshead Station ready to be evacuated to the countryside,

South Shields mums and young children on their way to being evacuated.

We're not downhearted! More South Shields children ready for a new adventure.

This happy study of evacuees from Heaton shows a school class setting out for a nature study 'somewhere in Northumberland'.

The wartime censor restricted the caption writer of this photograph to reference to a 'North-East unit' of Local Defence Volunteers.

The Lord Mayor of New-castle, Councillor A. D. Russell, inspecting men of the Home Guard attached to 'an engineering establishment in the North-East'.

According to the caption attached to this August 1940 photograph, this air-raid shelter saved the lives of four people 'during last night's raid over the North-East'.

These children of Temple Green, Gateshead, bring out the scrap metal they have collected towards the war effort.

Two 'fire watchers' on the roof of a Newcastle factory in January 1941.

Women were drafted into the armaments factories to produce much needed muntions. By November 1941 24-year-old Miss Cradock was an expert at gauging shells.

On Christmas Day 1941, this Newcastle family made a broadcast from Broadcasting House in Bridge Street on the BBC Forces Network programme *Absent Friends*.

The flotilla leader *HMS Kelly* passes the fishermen's pier – Lloyd's hailing jetty – heading out to sea for her trials off the Tyne in August 1939.

HMS Kelly after being hit by a torpedo in December 1940 while anti-mine-laying in the North Sea under the command of the young Louis Mountbatten. She was almost cut in two but refused to go down and miraculously made it back to the Tyne. She returned to action but her luck ran out and after being bombed by the Luftwaffe she went down off Crete with the loss of nine officers and 121 men.

Women welders return to work at Blyth Dry Dock Co Ltd.

Members of the Women's Land Army marching to a service at the County School of Agriculture, Houghall, on Farm Sunday in July 1943.

These women workers at the Elswick Works of Vickers are in patriotic mood.

These members of the Women's Timber Corps were working in the North-East of England in March 1943.

Bomb damage in Guildford Place after an air-raid on Newcastle in 1941.

Fireman play their hoses on the LNER Goods Station in New Bridge Street after an air-raid in September 1941.

Although suffering from a head wound this householder is seen carrying some of his belongings from his wrecked home in March 1943. Note the Union Flag among the rubble.

Members of the 50th (Northumbrian) Division parade down Grainger Street for the city's Victory Parade.

Crowded with sightseers these two lorries made excellent grandstands for the Victory Parade.

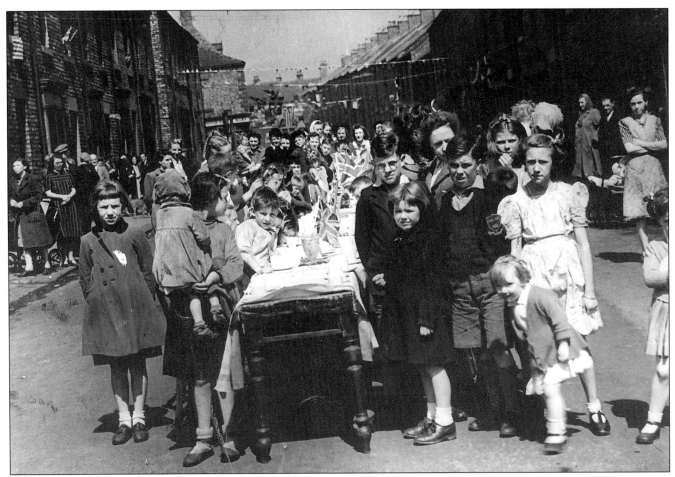

VE Day party in Trinity Street, North Shields.

Residents of Frank Street, Gateshead, join forces to make their own VE Day bonfire in May 1945.

All lit up. Gateshead's main VE Day bonfire at Wrekenton.

The day for which they'd all waited. VE Day street party at Lambert Square, Coxlodge.

The residents of Tamworth Road, Arthur's Hill, organised a street party and invited soldiers who were recovering from injury in Newcastle General Hospital to join them.

Stepping out in celebration. Wounded soldiers and local people in Tamworth Road, Arthur's Hill.

Exhibitions and Celebrations

The Prince of Wales, later King Edward VIII and then the Duke of Windsor, opens the North-East Coach Exhibition on Newcastle's Town Moor in 1929.

A corner of the exhibition site – the Palace of Industries which dwarfed visitors.

The Amusement Park at the North-East Coach Exhibition proved extremely popular during the hot weather.

One of the wonders of the North-East Coach Exhibition was this 70ft-high carillon with its 49 bells.

Industrial stands at the North-East Coach Exhibition, featuring some of the North-East's most stalwart companies.

Young visitors inspecting an RAF plane at the Empire Air Display held at Usworth Aerodrome in May 1935.

This giant Whitley bomber was the largest machine on view and attracted great interest during the Empire Air Display at Usworth RAF Station.

Salisbury Street, Byker, has long since been demolished but in September 1933 it was celebrating the title of Best Decorated Street.

Salisbury Street residents with tea, cakes and bunting – and a pennant announcing their victory.

In May 1935 these Tynesiders were celebrating the silver jubilee of King George V.

The Royal Proclamation announcing the accession to the throne by Queen Elizabeth II is read to the crowd waiting outside Gateshead Town Hall in February 1952.

Residents of Richard Street and Isabella Street add a touch of colour to their back lane lamp-posts in preparation for their Coronation Day party in June 1953.

These ladies of Pine Street, Newcastle, were determined that their street should be spick and span for the Coronation Day celebrations.

The residents of this Byker street had even whitewashed their walls in readiness for the Coronation Day street party.

Hawes Street, Byker, is ready for the party with flags, balloons and bunting.

Waving the flags for a new queen. A Coronation Day street party in Elswick.

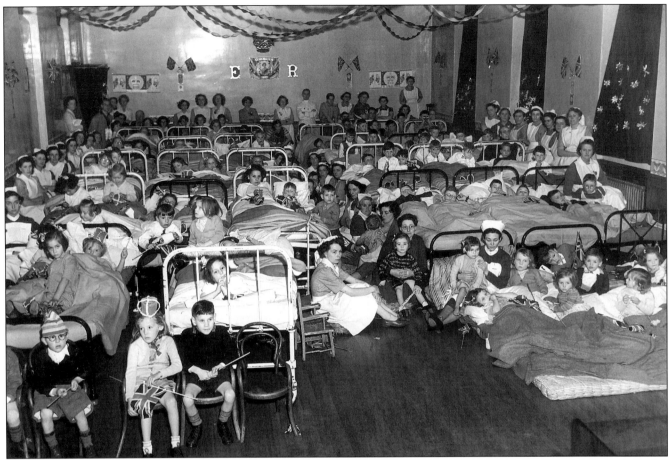

Over 100 patients at the Gosforth Sanderson Children's Hospital enjoyed the Coronation service and procession on television.

The climax to Newcastle's Coronation celebrations was the Lord Mayor's parade through the city's streets. Here the naval contingent are marching along Northumberland Street.

Judith Young tries out her Coronation beaker. She and Roy Dredge were at a Coronation party held at the Percy Hedley School for Spastic Children at Forest Hall, Newcastle.

Decorated motorcycles formed part of the Tynemouth Coronation Carnival Parade.

Not so much horse-power but these decorated cycles were just as much a part of the Tynemouth Coronation Carnival Parade which started at the Queen Victoria School.

From all over the county miners and their families followed the lodge banners into Durham City for the 69th 'Big Meeting', the Miners' Gala, in July 1952.

Royal Visitors

The Prince of Wales (later King Edward VII) rides past Bainbridge's Store in Market Street on his way to open the Royal Victoria Infirmary in 1900.

The Prince of Wales (later King Edward VIII) inspects a guard of honour at Alnwick in July 1923.

The Prince of Wales, the man who was to become King Edward VIII and then abdicate, inspects nurses at Newcastle Orthopaedic Hospital.

King George V during his visit to Newcastle in November 1928. He was accompanied by Queen Mary when he visited the city to officially open the new Tyne Bridge.

King George V and Queen Mary pictured with Newcastle civic dignitaries during their November 1928 visit to the city.

The Prince of Wales returned to Tyneside in April 1932 and is pictured here leaving a house at Rye Hill.

The Prince of Wales arrives at Washington Station during his visit which included a tour of the Durham Social Services Centre.

The Duchess of York, later Queen Elizabeth the Queen Mother, tries her hand at bowls during a visit she and her husband made to the North-East in August 1936. This photograph was taken at Kibblesworth Miners's Welfare Ground.

In February 1939 the Duchess of York returned to the North-East as Queen Elizabeth with her husband, then King George VI. Here they are arriving to open the new Medical School in Newcastle.

The King and Queen meet local dignitaries upon their arrival at Newcastle General Hospital.

Queen Elizabeth watches girls working at a factory on the Team Valley Trading Estate in Gateshead. King George VI is in the middle of the trio in the background.

Queen Elizabeth II meets some smiling faces at Hexham in July 1974.

Crowds welcome the Royal Yacht *Britannia* as it enters the Tyne in July 1977, the Queen's silver jubilee year.

A hand holding a posey pushes towards the Queen as she goes walkabout in Eldon Square in July 1977.

The Queen and Prince Phillip leave the Eldon Square shopping centre.

These Gateshead ladies left no one in doubt about their feelings during the 1977 royal visit.

A smiling Princess of Wales at Dr Barnado's Centre for the Unemployed in Whitley Bay in July 1988.

A smiling Queen at Cramlington High School playing fields.

Some Other Well-Known Faces

Sir Oswald Mosley, leader of the British Fascist Movement, pictured (second left) with some of his followers at the Haymarket in July 1934 following a rally on the Town Moor.

Mr James Denyer, director of Newcastle Airport, looks on as Alderman James Cunningham, chairman of the North-East Regional Airport Committee, chats with Prime Minister Harold Wilson on his arrival at the airport in February 1967.

Premier Harold Wilson on the balcony of the County Hotel in Durham, waving to crowds below marching to the Racecourse in the early 1970s. It had become a tradition for the serving Labour leader to attend the Durham Miners' Gala.

US President Jimmy Carter receives the Freedom of the City of Newcastle in 1977.

Jimmy Carter meets the crowds outside Newcastle Civic Centre. He opened his speech with the words: "Howay the Lads!"

In 1969, T. Dan Smith, then chairman of the Northern Economic Planning Council, explains points in the strategy for priority developments in the Tyneside and Wearside areas. As leader of Newcastle City Council he was all-powerful and promised to revitalise Newcastle as the 'Brasilia of the North'. But with two others, Durham County Council boss and trades union baron Andrew Cunningham, and failed architect John Poulson, he was jailed following a sensational trial after their massive corruption was exposed.

Sir Harry Lauder, the great Scottish entertainer, greets the daughter of a former co-star, Bessie Featherstone, at the Empire Theatre, Newcastle, in 1937.

Andy Cunningham (left) is pictured here with his co-driver Duke Brewer of Pickering after they had beaten T. Dan Smith in a race at the England Steam Traction Rally at Birtley. Cunningham betrayed the working class whose interests he claimed to represent and, like Smith, was sent to prison.

Rock Around the Clock star Bill Hayley reads a special *Chronicle* edition published in honour of his visit to Newcastle.

Marji Wallace, Miss World 1973, received a pop star's welcome when she visited the North-East in January 1974. She presented two buses provided by the Variety Club of Great Britain for use by needy youngsters. Two months later she was stripped of her crown after complaints about her lifestyle, including associating with George Best and Tom Jones among others!

Police keep back crowds during the visit to South Shields by Muhammad Ali in 1977.

Muhammad Ali spars with 19-year-old Les Close at Grainger Park Boys' Club, Scotswood.

In the early 1960s Newcastle was visited by the notorious Kray twins, pictured with big brother Charlie. They arrived at Central Station and booked into the Royal Station Hotel. Legend has it that Newcastle police delivered to them a railway timetable with the time of the next train out of town underlined. They left!

Perhaps not such a familiar face to 21st-century Tynesiders but 75 years ago he was well-known in the city. Mr Fryer, manager of the local Broadcasting Station was leaving Newcastle to take over at Bournemouth and is here pictured being presented with a silver cigar case and silver matching box on behalf of the Children's Fairy Flower League.

Leisure and Pleasure

There were always big turnouts for the regular Sunday afternoon band concerts in Leazes Park at the turn of the century.

In 1909 the star attraction at the Spanish City funfair in Whitley Bay was the water chute.

In those long, hot summers of Edwardian England, the Lady's Steps at Swalwell, near Gateshead, was a popular picnic spot and a place for a cool paddle.

A summer's day at Whitley Bay in the years before World War One.

The great Dan Leno as the Dame in the pantomime Widow Twankey at the Theatre Royal, Newcastle.

A happy scene at the New Orleans Club in Newcastle in 1959.

Leader Herbie Butch wrote many ballads and skiffle numbers for the Hebburn-based Cougars Skiffle Group, pictured here in 1958.

In 1958 the Dicer Rhythm Boys took the North-East scene by storm. They are fruiterer Stan Holford (string bass), fruiterer Sam Holford (drums), armature winder Arny Clarke (guitar) and boot repairer Rod Blair (guitar).

Pop star Adam Faith performing at Newcastle's Dolca Vita nightclub in May 1965.

Lindisfarne, the local group who found fame with their song *Fog On The Tyne* (1974) which became the area's 'anthem'.

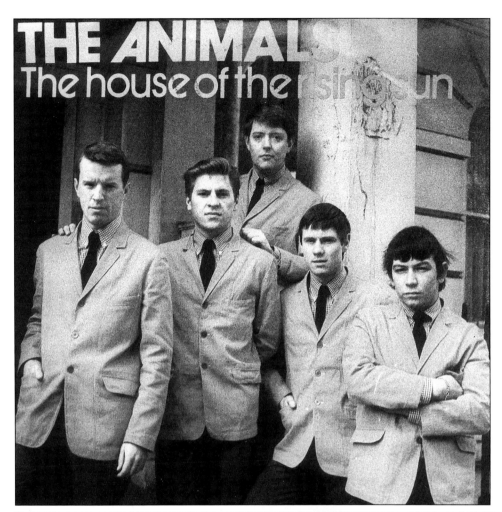

Tyneside Group The Animals. Left to right are John Steel, Alan Price, Chas Chandler, Hilton Valentine and Eric Burdon.

In 1966, James Bolam and Rodney Bewes were BBC TV's *The Likely Lads*, the archetypal Geordie lads after beer and birds. The series was relaunched as *Whatever Happened To The Likely Lads?*

In 1975 James Bolam played Jack Ford in another BBC TV series based in the North-East, *When The Boat Comes In*. Here Bolam is pictured with actress Susan Jameson who played Betty Seaton.

In 1971 these girls from the Louise James Agency appeared in a spectacular fashion show produced in Newcastle for C & A. The entire team of 11 girls, three male models and four children plus DJ and compère Bill Steele came from Newcastle. From left to right are Clare Rowden, Lynn Evans, Ann Dover, Jennifer Moss, Caroline Bowden and Simmi.

Singing star Gracie Fields drew a huge crowd when she opened Black's Regal Cinema – later the Odeon – at Gateshead in 1937.

The plush interior of Black's Regal Cinema pictured in February 1937.

Newcastle's four-screen Odeon Cinema pictured in April 1980.

The Odeon packed to the brim with 1,200 children and their parents in December 1984.

In 1990 the National Garden Festival was held on a 200-acre site along the banks of the Tyne at Gateshead. Here a monorail glides over a model of the Forth Bridge.

Ships ahoy! A forest of masts during the visit of the Tall Ships to the Tyne in 1993.

Happiest Days of Their Lives?

Robert Emerson, a mineral water manufacturer, started his new works in George Street, Newcastle, by giving breakfast to 500 poor children in the basement of his factory *c*.1890.

Pencils poised, this 1909 class at Westgate Road School look a well-behaved lot.

These young ladies comprised the sixth form of Church High School in 1913.

A class of Westgate Hill Council School pictured *c*.1918.

Maypole dancing at the Park Infant School, Whitley Bay, in 1936.

Boy trainees get their lamps before going below at Ashington Colliery's underground school in April 1942.

Now where? These Newcastle boys (from left to right) Kenneth Jeffrey (14), Albert Fawcett (12) and Henry Fairgreaves (14) had been on a camping holiday at Ovingham. Now they consult their map while their dog waits patiently for them to make up their minds.

Headmaster Mr J. E. Robson marking some of his juniors' exercise books at Whittingham Church of England School in June 1954,

Children playing on partly demolished houses at Back Newcombe Street, Elswick, Newcastle in October 1957.

These pupils at Hamsteels Church of England School look properly attentive in October 1955.

In 1960 these pupils at Dame Allan's School were preparing for their examinations in the school library.

King's College research assistants Maureen Thompson and Pamela Murgetroyd study some tropical ferns in a greenhouse in 1963. King's College later became Newcastle University.

Secretaries in the making at Cramlington High School in May 1973.

Children in the playground at Waterhouses School in October 1962.

An impromptu cricket match in progress at Ravenswood School in July 1969.

Youngsters try out their soccer skills at Craigside Junior School in July 1969.

The doors open for business at West Jesmond School in March 1979 and at least one young pupil looks pleased as he gives the *Chronicle* cameraman a thumbs-up.

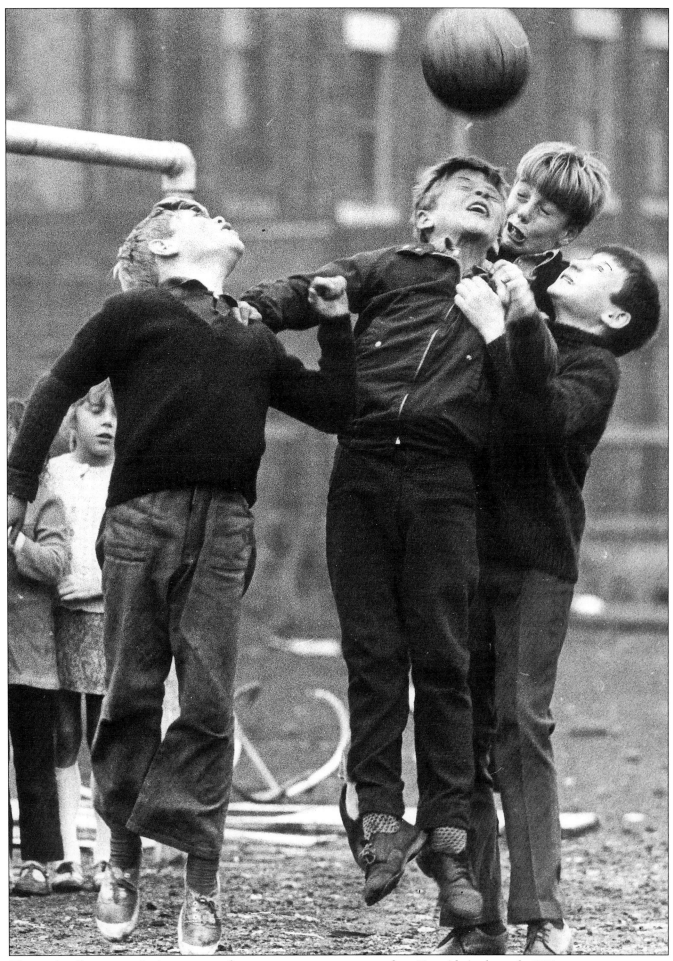

These schoolboys are enjoying a game of soccer on some waste ground on Tyneside in the early 1970s.

Sun, Rain and Snow

Sun worshippers enjoy a golden day at Whitley Bay in July 1971.

In the scorching summer of 1976 these two ladies enjoyed a paddle at Tynemouth.

Not quite the beach but still enjoyable: office workers relax in the sun on the grass of St John's Church, just off Grainger Road, in June 1973.

Back to 1976 and Brian Lewis tries a rain dance to end the drought.

It's often thought that every summer in Edwardian England was a golden one. But in 1910 there was so much rain that Jesmond Road looked like a swollen river.

In August 1975 non-stop rain in the North-East led to some of the worst flooding in living memory. The Tyne burst its banks in several places and at one spot has risen by some 16 feet.

In February 1929 the Tyne was frozen solid at Hexham Bridge. Over a century earlier, in January 1914, the Tyne was so deeply frozen at Newcastle that an 'ice fair' was celebrated on the river.

Soldiers help to clear Gallowgate after the great snowfall of March 1941. A trolley bus is just one traffic casualty of the great 'white out'.

All hands to the shovel. Snow clearing in Newcastle city centre in March 1941.

The Great North Road, heading towards Barras Bridge, in the big freeze of March 1941.

In February 1978 traffic was at a standstill on Forth Banks, Newcastle. It was a case of push and shove to get to work in another severe winter.

Disasters

The face of a hero – the first rescuer to reach West Stanley pit's Busty seam when the 1909 colliery disaster claimed the lives of 168 men.

Relatives pictured with pitiful bundles of food for the 'canny lads' who would never be rescued after the Montague Pit disaster of 30 March 1925.

Women and children wait for news of their loved ones after the Montague Pit disaster.

A vehicle of the Durham and Northumberland Collieries Fire and Rescue Brigade is surrounded by local people waiting news.

A funeral procession moves slowly through Scotswood after the Montague Pit disaster. The final death toll was 38 men and boys which included Thomas Machum who was just 14.

How a contemporary newspaper reported the 'Great Fire of Newcastle'. In December 1919 fire broke out in Cross House, an 80ft-high building in Westgate Road. Twelve people perished and many more would have died but for the heroics of the fire brigade.

Marjorie Stabler (above) was a young girl when she witnessed the Cross House Fire.

In 1996, Marjorie Stabler was present when there was a re-enactment of the Cross House Fire of almost 80 years earlier.

This open-cab bus with its solid rubber wheels careered through the parapet of Swalwell Bridge during World War One.

In February 1915, a runaway tram went out of control at Bensham Bank and killed four people.

In the early hours of 7 May 1969 the night sleeper the *Aberdonian*, left Newcastle. On the notorious Morpeth curve, disaster struck and five passengers and a ticket collector were killed. Some 121 passengers were injured, 19 of them seriously.

Beds and mattresses from the ill-fated *Aberdonian* are strewn over the track surrounded by the tangled remains of the express train.

Police investigate the crash of the *Merry Hampton,* a powerful Pacific locomotive which was pulling nine coaches and a restaurant car as she neared Cramlington during the 1926 General Strike. It was the worst case of sabotage during the ten-day strike and eight Northumberland miners were jailed for between four and eight years for causing the derailment.

In Protest

Suffragette Emily Wilding Davison, from Morpeth, threw her self under the king's horse at the 1913 Derby and died two days later from terrible wounds.

Emily Pankhurst, leader of the Suffragette Movement, pictured holding a book at a South Shields by-election.

A group of Suffragettes recently released from prison are pictured at Newcastle Central Station. The tall girl on the left is Charlotte Marsh of Newcastle.

Protesting Suffragettes march down Northumberland Street *c.*1906.

Newspaper cutting reporting the clash between South Shields policemen and rioting Arab seamen in 1930, when sailing jobs were denied to the area's ethnic community due to union restrictions.

FIERCE RIOT AT SHIELDS.

POLICEMEN STABBED IN BATTLE WITH ARABS.

27 ARRESTS.

FOUR "MINORITY" LEADERS AMONG THEM.

RIOTING by Arabs at the Mill Dam, South Shields, yesterday afternoon, produced a pitched battle with the police. Four constables were stabbed and 20 Arabs injured.

Two of the policemen were seriously wounded, and one— Plain Clothes Officer Gash—was reported this morning to be in a critical condition.

Early this morning 27 arrests had been made, including 21 Arabs and four leaders of the Seamen's Minority Movement.

Police officers move forward towards the rioting Arab seamen.

One seaman is arrested and marched away by local police.

Local workers listen to an address from a union official. Four constables were stabbed and 20 Arabs injured after protests from the Seamen's Minority Movement.

Soup kitchens were set up all over the country to feed strikers during the 1926 General Strike. This one was at Brough Park.

The scene in Howard Street, North Shields, in October 1932 after police had drawn batons to disperse unemployed local men who were protesting.

The Jarrow Crusade – the so-called Hunger March of 1932 – enters London with its petition calling for work.

The Jarrow marchers making their way to Marble Arch.

The protesters march on in the rain towards Hyde Park. After initial hostility the men found a warm reception in many of the southern towns through which they passed.

In March 1969, Tyneside teachers staged a protest in support of a pay rise.

In August 1971 this small protester's placard told its own story. Six-year-old Tony Thompson had been hurt in a car accident outside his home Ventor Gardens, Whitley Bay. Now he wanted to make his street safe for other children.

January 1971 and Tyneside shipyard workers held a mass meeting in protest at the Government's Industrial Relations Bill.

Fists are raised defiantly as Swan Hunter men leave a meeting at Hebburn in July 1975.

In August 1975, five thousand Tyneside shipyard workers voted to take on their bosses and the Government over pay. At a stormy lunchtime meeting they elected to reject a company pay offer and remain on strike.

Still in the summer of 1975 and it's a unanimous decision by Federation Brewery workers in Newcastle to carry on their strike.

In 1978 hands shot up as 3,500 engineering workers on the verge of a pre-Christmas strike, voted to accept a new deal which would give them the highest minimum wage on Tyneside. The mass meeting of NEI Parsons employees bowed to pressure put on by James Callaghan's government's decision to put a £200 million generator contract back into the melting pot.

In February 1979 these Tyneside social workers, who had been on strike for six months, picketed a meeting as councillors arrived.

Police and strikers battle at Ellington Colliery during the 1984 coal miners' strike.

A barrier goes up in flames at Whittle Colliery during the 1984 miners' strike.

Following United

Newcastle United's first-team staff at the start of the 20th century. Back row (left to right): T. Dodd (trainer), J. Rogers, C. Burgess, M. Kingsley, J. Peddie, J. Fraser, Cockburn (groundsman). Middle row: A. MacFarlane, F. Haywood, C. Watts, D. Gardner, T. Niblo, F. G. Watt (secretary). Front: E. Allen, A. Aitken, T. Ghee, A. Gardner, J. Carr. Frank Watt was Newcastle's secretary for 36 years and was a great influence on the club's rise.

Newcastle United at the start of the 1905-06 season. The previous year they won the League championship for the first time. Back row (left to right): A. McCombie, G. T. Milne (director), J. W. Bell (director), G. G. Archibald (director), J. Lawrence. Second row: R. Oliver (director), P. Oliver (director), J. Carr, W. McCracken, J. Cameron (chairman), Jos Bell (vice-chairman), P. McWilliam, J. McClarence, J. Graham (director). Seated: F. G. Watt (secretary), A. Aitken, J. Rutherford, J. Howie, A. Appleyard, R. Orr, A. Gosnell, J. Q, McPherson (trainer). On ground: C. Veitch, A. Gardner.

Aerial action from a match between Newcastle and Woolwich Arsenal in front of 50,000 fans at St James's Park in 1906.

This photograph of United's 1907-08 playing staff also shows some of the trophies won by the club. In the middle is the huge Sheriff of London's Charity Shield, forerunner of the FA Charity Shield now traditionally competed for by the Premiership winners and the FA Cup holders. Also on show from left to right are the Northumberland Senior Cup, Football League championship trophy, Royal Victoria Infirmary Cup, Tynemouth Infirmary Cup and the North-Eastern League championship trophy.

Newcastle United in 1910-11, the season they beat Barnsley 2-0 in the FA Cup Final at Old Trafford after a drawn first game at the Crystal Palace. Back row (left to right): R. Waugh, D. Willis, G. Hardy (assistant trainer), A. Anderson, J. Finlay. Inset is J. Rutherford. Second row: W. McCracken, W. Low, C. Veitch, P. McWilliam, T. Whitson. Seated: A. Duncan, J. Howie, A. Shepherd, J. Stewart, A. Higgins, G. Wilson. On ground: F. G. Watt (secretary), J. Lawrence, J. Q. McPherson (trainer).

Newcastle United in 1913-14. Back row (left to right): T. Goodwill, T. Curry, G.Harrison, D. Dunglinson. Second row: W. Liddle, J. Carr, J. Q. McPherson (trainer), J. Finlay, T. Hughes, R. Hewison, A. McCombie (assistant trainer), J. Spink, T. Cooper. Third row: F. G. Watt junior (assistant secretary), J. King, J. Carr, T. Grey, W. Low, T. Hall, R. Little, J. McDonald, Frank G. Watt (secretary). Seated: W. Warren, C. Veitch, W. Hibbert, J. Hay, A. Higgins, Alderman Archibald (chairman), W. McCracken, G. Wilson, A. Shepherd, F. Hudspeth, T. Whitson. On ground: S. Hardy, S. Blake, J. Alderson, J. Lawrence, T. Lowes.

Newcastle United in 1924, as they embarked on what would be a successful FA Cup campaign which ended with victory over Aston Villa at Wembley. Back row (left to right): J. Q. McPherson (trainer), E. Mooney, N. Harris, F. Hudspeth, R. Clark, C. Spencer, A. McCombie (assistant trainer), Frank G. Watt (secretary). Seated: J. Low, T. Curry, W. Hampson, W. Bradley, S, Russell, T. McDonald, W. Cowan. On ground:W. Gibson and S. Seymour.

Hughie Gallacher heads another goal for Newcastle United. Gallacher, a Scottish international, joined the Magpies in December 1925 and went on to score 143 goals in only 174 games for them, a staggering return. He later played for Chelsea and Derby, amassing over 400 senior goals altogether, but his private life was a disaster and in June 1957, when facing charges of cruelty to his son, he ended his life in front of an express train not far from his Gateshead home.

United supporters at the Central Railway Station in February 1932, on their way to Newcastle's FA Cup tie at Southport. The sides had drawn 1-1 on Tyneside and that was also the score at Haig Avenue. But in the second replay, at Hillsborough, Newcastle made no mistake with a 9-0 scoreline to send themselves further along the road to another Wembley appearance.

Newcastle's Jack Allen scores one of the most controversial goals in the history of the FA Cup Final, when he heads home Jimmy Richardson's cross against Arsenal at Wembley in 1932.

This photograph suggests that the ball was over the goal-line before Richardson swung it back into the middle.

Newcastle with skipper Jimmy Nelson 'in the chair' with the FA Cup. Others in the picture (from left to right) are McMenemy, Richardson, McInroy, Davidson, Allen, Weaver, Boyd and Lang.

The triumphant Newcastle team return to Tyneside to be greeted by tens of thousands of deliriously happy Geordie fans after the Magpies' 1932 Cup victory.

Here he looks more like a politician, but Jimmy Nelson has just skippered Newcastle United to FA Cup glory.

During World War Two, Newcastle, like many other clubs, fielded a mixture of regular players and guest stars. This group includes Albert Stubbins (second from left), Tot Smith, Charlie Wayman and, far right, a youthful Jackie Milburn. Stubbins went on to greater things in Liverpool's colours.

August 1950 and former Magpies star Hughie Gallacher prepares to referee a ladies' football match between Hazlerigg Women's Supporters Club and Dudley Ladies' Physical Culture Club.

Not a sight to be broadcast today but in the 1940s the dangers of smoking were not so evident. Newcastle United star Jackie Milburn takes a light from full-back Duggie Graham.

Jackie Milburn scores Newcastle's second goal at Wembley in 1951 to clinch an FA Cup Final victory over Blackpool.

George Robledo heads the goals which gave Newcastle victory over Arsenal in the 1952 FA Cup Final.

'Pop' Robson goes full-length to head in Newcastle's second goal in their 4-0 Inter Cities Fairs Cup win over the Dutch side Feyenoord in 1968. The Magpies won this first-round tie 4-2 on aggregate.

This time Robson (8) is in action against Sporting Lisbon in the second round of the Fairs Cup in November 1968. United won this game 1-0 and the tie 2-1 on aggregate.

Robson's second-minute goal against Real Zaragoza at St James's Park set the scene for a 2-1 Fairs Cup win and although the aggregate over two legs was 4-4, United won on the away-goals rule.

In March 1969, United beat Vitoria Setubal 5-1 in the Fairs Cup quarter-finals and won 6-4 on aggregate. Here the goal feast gets under way in the 23rd minute as left winger Alan Foggan heads home a centre from right-back John Craggs.

Jackie Sinclair scores the second goal against Rangers in the Fairs Cup semi-final second leg at Gallowgate. United won 2-0 on the night after a goalless first leg at Ibrox.

In the 1969 Fairs Cup Final first leg against the Hungarian side Ujpest Dozsa at St James's Park, leading scorer Bryan 'Pop' Robson is foiled on this occasion by Ujpest goalkeeper Szentimihalyi.

Big Welsh striker Wyn Davies puts Ujpest Dozsa under pressure.

Bobby Moncur (6) celebrates his goal against Ujpest Dozsa. United won 3-0 and then triumphed 3-2 in the away leg to lift the Fairs Cup with a 6-2 aggregate.

Bob Moncur, manager Joe Harvey and striker Jim Scott pictured after the Magpies' home win had surely put the tie beyond the reach of the Hungarian club.

Jubilant United supporters after their side had made the trip to Hungary a formality.

'Pop' Robson, now playing for West Ham United, tries to break through the Newcastle defence at St James's Park in April 1971 with full-back Frank Clark in attendance.

Bob Moncur stops Arsenal's Ray Kennedy at St James's Park in March 1972.

John Tudor and Malcolm Macdonald turn away to celebrate a goal against Leeds United in 1972. The crestfallen Leeds players are Paul Reaney and David Harvey.

Liverpool's Emlyn Hughes and Ray Clemence combine to keep out Newcastle's Jim Smith at St James's Park in April 1973.

An unhappy moment for Norwich City goalkeeper Kevin Keelan as he is challenged by Newcastle's Alan Gowling at Gallowgate in October 1975.

Missed it! Charlton Athletic goalkeeper Nicky Jones is in trouble as Newcastle's Peter Wythe puts in a hefty challenge at St James's Park in March 1979.

Chris Waddle in action against Manchester City in October 1983. Peter Beardsley looks on. The Magpies won the match 5-0

Three of a kind: United's international stars David McCreery, Terry McDermott and Kevin Keegan try to sort it out against Chelsea in March 1984.

There is a helping hand from the law as Kevin Keegan struggles to keep his feet on a lap of honour after Newcastle United are promoted back to the top flight in May 1984.

Paul Gascoigne's shot hits the back of the net after a mix-up between Southampton's David Armstrong and Peter Shilton in March 1987.

One of the first of the foreign 'imports'. Brazilian star Mirandinha wreaks havoc in a Newcastle shirt in October 1987.

Other Sporting Days

When ladies showed an ankle and no more. A race at the Shotley Bridge Institute Sports Day in 1911.

Princess Wah Letka congratulating Tom Payne, the walker and 'musical athlete' after his non-stop walk to Morpeth and back in September 1921. A. S. Reeve, a Newcastle journalist, raced him on the 30-mile round trip, being giving a mile and a half start.

J. Robinson of the Early Birds was the oldest cyclist to ride from Newcastle to Barnard Castle for the North-Eastern meeting in May 1932.

Speedway star Ivan Mauger came to Tyneside from New Zealand in 1963 and three years later won the European and World crowns before switching to Belle Vue where he won five more world titles.

A fine action study of Ivan Mauger in action at Brough Park.

Gosforth prop Ray McCloughlin pictured (above left) in 1971 when he was about to embark on the British Lions tour to New Zealand. Another former Gosforth star, full-back Bill Charlton (right) who later coached Morpeth. McCloughlin and Charlton were instrumental in the Gosforth club's rise through the 1960s.

Telford Moralee of Percy Park is chaired by his teammates as he holds the Northumberland Senior Cup in 1949.

Steve Gustard breaks through for Gosforth against Percy Park in December 1983. Gustard led Northumberland to the County Championship in 1981 with a team comprising mostly Gosforth players.

Gosforth golfer Alan Thirlwell won two English Championships and countless England caps as well as a Walker Cup place. He is pictured here in May 1955.

Alan Thirlwell drives from the second tee at Ponteland during the 1967 Northumberland Championship.

Jimmy Hayes (left) is congratulated by Alan Thirlwell after winning the 1965 Northumberland Championship at Arcot Hall.

David Curry of Prudhoe was a gifted amateur golfer who dominated the North-East scene in the 1980s before becoming a professional. He won junior and full international caps, a Walker Cup place and the 1986 British Amateur title.

Winner of the 1965 Morpeth to Newcastle race for the Journal Cup is Jim Alder of Morpeth, who set five records at various checkpoints and went on to win the race in record time. He went on to win the race five more times and gained many international honours including gold in the 1966 Commonwealth Games marathon. He also held world records over 30 kilometres.

Steve Cram (113), Gary Staines (107) and Mike McLeod pictured during the Gateshead 10-kilometre race. In 1985 Cram smashed world records for the mile, 1,500 metres and 2,000 metres within the space of 19 days. In all, his list of titles and records read like a world athletics 'hall of fame'. McLeod, too – 'the Elswick Express' had his share of fame and lifted silver in the 1984 Olympics 10,000 after his medal had been elevated from bronze following a Finnish runner failing a drugs test.

Brendan Foster of Gateshead Harriers takes an early lead in the English National Cross Country Championships at London's Parliament Hill Fields in 1977. Following in the footsteps of Jim Alder, Foster set new standards and not only put Gateshead and the North-East on the athletics map but became an icon in British sport with a host of national and world records and medals in European, Commonwealth and Olympic competition.